How to Write Your UCAS Personal Statement and Get into University: The Ultimate Guide

MOHAN-PAL SINGH CHANDAN

authorHOUSE®

AuthorHouse™ UK Ltd.
1663 Liberty Drive
Bloomington, IN 47403 USA
www.authorhouse.co.uk
Phone: 0800.197.4150

© 2014 Mohan-pal Singh Chandan. All rights reserved.

No part of this book may be reproduced, stored in a retrieval system, or transmitted by any means without the written permission of the author.

Published by AuthorHouse   05/09/2014

ISBN: 978-1-4969-7913-1 (sc)
ISBN: 978-1-4969-7914-8 (e)

Any people depicted in stock imagery provided by Thinkstock are models, and such images are being used for illustrative purposes only. Certain stock imagery © Thinkstock.

Because of the dynamic nature of the Internet, any web addresses or links contained in this book may have changed since publication and may no longer be valid. The views expressed in this work are solely those of the author and do not necessarily reflect the views of the publisher, and the publisher hereby disclaims any responsibility for them.

For all students in the noble pursuit of higher education

Table of Contents

A note from the author — ix

The basics — 1
Introduction — 1
    How to make decisions — 2
    Sources of information (SOI) — 5
    Managing your money — 7
    International applicants — 8
UCAS — 8
    UCAS timeline — 9

Decisions, decisions — 11
What career? — 11
    Making a career plan — 14
What course? — 15
    Course content — 15
    Course structure — 15
    Course assessment — 16
    Course learning style — 16
    Accredited courses — 17
    Academic requirements and predicted grades — 17
    Work experience and other requirements — 18
Which university? — 19
    Make a shortlist — 20

Your application 21
The Personal Statement 21
   Overview 21
   What they are looking for 22
   Do's and Don'ts for UCAS Personal Statements 23
   Section 1: introduction 26
   Section 2: experience that makes you the ideal candidate 27
   Section 3: broader experience 30
   Section 4: conclusion 31
   How to begin writing it 32
   How to sell yourself 35
   How to refine it 36
Interviews 38
Aptitude tests 42

Subject-specific advice 43
   Medicine 43
   Dentistry 55
   Nursing, Pharmacy and other health or social care degrees 56
   Law 59
   Economics 61
   Business Studies and Management 63
   Psychology 65
   Engineering 67
   Computer Science 68
   Media and Journalism 69
   Music 72
   English and other academic subjects 74
   Foreign languages 77
   Teaching 79
   Post-graduate courses 87

A final note from the author 89

A note from the author

I went to a high-ranking UK secondary school but still felt unsupported with my own UCAS application. My school's career guidance services have now improved dramatically, but at that time I had to rely on family and friends for the support I needed. I then thought; if I am struggling, surely there are thousands of other people also not getting the guidance they deserve. I came to know many international applicants for whom English was a second language and came to understand the difficulties they faced as well as the varying quality of guidance available to them.

During university it became my ambition to get a team of experts together and share our knowledge of the university application process with as many people as possible, giving one-to-one coaching and guidance. The first stage of this was PersonalStatementChecker.com, where we selected a team of graduates from top UK universities to critique, edit and write detailed reports on applicants' personal statements and answer their questions about the application process.

This book is the next stage for our team and is the culmination of over 25 years of combined experience in helping people with university applications. I would personally like to thank those who contributed to this project, without whom it would not have been possible: Caroline, Alida, Satbir and Preety. I would also like to thank my wife Simran for all her tireless support and encouragement and our loving family for all the guidance and motivation they provide.

Mohan-pal Singh Chandan

The basics

Introduction

You're reading this book because you've made what is probably the most important decision in life so far; to apply for a degree. This can be a confusing and anxious time in life with so many decisions to make and so many opinions to take into account.

With fees of £9000 per year, a new range of private colleges and universities, and increasing competition for the top courses, it is now more challenging than ever to get into the higher education course you want. However, if you are determined, prepared, and have the right advice, you will give yourself the best chances of securing an offer.

The personal statement is now more important than ever. In a recent survey, admissions tutors rated good written English and a passion for the subject as some of the most important non-academic parts of the entire UCAS application. The personal statement is often your only real chance to demonstrate these skills and traits to admissions tutors, so it is important to stand out.

Furthermore, figuring out what course to apply for and where you want your education and career to take you are some pretty difficult decisions to make. Careers advisors in schools and colleges struggle to keep up-to-date with the latest developments. As the team at PersonalStatementChecker.com include subject-specialists from a wide range of fields, we are able to stay abreast of new trends and give you the knowledge you need to make informed choices about your future.

At PersonalStatementChecker.com we have many years of experience with offering personal statement support and careers guidance for people applying to university. Many of our team have spent time with admissions tutors to establish exactly what they look for when selecting candidates.

This book aims to increase your chances of securing an offer at your first choice of university, by collating the most important pearls of wisdom for the personal statement and the UCAS application as a whole based upon our extensive experience. It's intended to supplement other sources of advice for the UCAS application as well as provide detailed and comprehensive guidance for the personal statement. Our specialists in different subject areas have also contributed chapters with information that is important for applicants to specific subjects.

80% of customers in our latest annual customer survey secured places at their first choice university, whilst the other 20% still secured offers or interviews. With the expert assistance of our team, their personal statements gave them an edge in being considered by some of the most competitive UK universities.

We hope you find this useful and wish you the best of luck with your application!

How to make decisions

You might already know that you want to be a human rights lawyer working 3 days a week in your own firm, 1 and a half days a week doing voluntary legal aid work and spending one morning a week on your private yacht. You might already know exactly what experience you'll need to get to that stage, which Law degree you want to study, where you want to study it, what the entry requirements are, and what your Plan B is if you don't meet the requirements.

If this sounds familiar, you are probably that rare breed of person who is already extremely good at making decisions. However, for most of us, deciding about university can be a difficult and confusing process so it's useful to spend a minute to step back and think about how you're going to make these decisions. Here are a few Do's and Don'ts:

Do

- Research everything: Knowledge is power. The more information you have, the more evidence you will have to help you make decisions. Making decisions without information is like trying to navigate without a map. More about this in the next chapter.

- Write it down: If you keep notes and lists you can always come back to it if you've forgotten.

- Think about what is important for you: Is staying at home for university the most important factor for you for financial or other reasons? Do you want to go somewhere with great nightlife? Would you rather study the course you enjoy learning about or something that is better linked to the career you want? Think about what you want from your career, and from your life in general. What do you want to achieve? Think about what the important factors are for you and see which of your options ticks all the right boxes

- Use the process of elimination: Most people find it helpful to look at all of your options side-by-side and eliminate the least favourable ones.

- Be realistic: If you have achieved C's and B's at AS level and don't have any relevant work experience it will be really difficult for you to apply to the most competitive universities or for a competitive course such as medicine or economics. On the other side of the spectrum, if you have very high grades, have plenty of experience and a real passion for the subject, studying at one of the best universities should be well within your grasp; don't just apply for "backup" university courses.

- Realise you may not find the perfect solution: You may have missed out on the grades for your dream degree but don't be disheartened. If you keep an open mind, you'll find something else for sure.

- Speak to people but make the decision yourself: There will be many people in your life who you can turn to for advice about the decision but don't let someone make the decision for you. It's your application, you will be studying the course and it will be your future. We often meet applicants whose parents told them to apply for medicine but the applicant either doesn't want to study medicine or actually doesn't even know what they want. If this describes you, don't worry, now is the time to do your research. You'll soon figure out what to do if you have enough information.

- Think long-term: "Begin with the end in mind" is one of Stephen Covey's "7 habits of highly effective people". Think about which of your options will give you the best outlook in 5, 10, 20 or even 40 years' time.

- Make a Plan B: A lot of people don't really think about what they'll do if they don't get offers from the courses they apply for, or if they don't meet the grade requirements. Take some time now to plan what you will do if things don't work out the way you wanted them to the first time round. Look at UCAS Clearing, UCAS Extra and other options such as applying next year, gaining more experience or alternative careers.

Don't

- Get lost in the decision-making process: A lot of people suffer from "analysis paralysis". If you find yourself going in circles, take some time out. There's not much that a cup of tea can't solve.

- Be afraid: if you've used lots of sources of information and thought about these clearly, you will have made a good decision. Trust yourself.

- Delay: Some people see making decisions about university as a mountain that is too big to start tackling today and put it off. Break it down into little chunks and start today. You'll thank yourself later.

- Get stuck on an idea without any information: Someone may have told you to study pharmacy but you have no idea what the course is like, what you need to do to get in, or what life as a pharmacist is like. Do the research first and then you'll be able to decide for yourself if it's a good option for you.

Sources of information (SOI)

Getting opinions from other people is important and very useful but you should make sure they are reliable sources. For some of us, our parents, siblings or cousins may be people we look up to and trust for good advice. Other people could be friends, teachers, or other people in our lives. PersonalStatementChecker.com editors can also offer advice alongside their personal statement review service and people find that their opinions are very useful due to the sheer amount of specialist experience they have.

Here's a list of sources of information that you should use when making decisions about university. We'll refer to these throughout the book.

- PersonalStatementChecker.com advisors: experienced professionals in the field, who possess a fountain of knowledge about courses, careers, the personal statement and can offer advice on all aspects of the application.

- UCAS website: the best place for information about the application process and an overview of individual courses.

- University websites and prospectuses: best for entry requirements and to find out what they are looking for in the personal statement.

- Online careers advice sources: www.whatpeopledo.co.uk is a great site that includes career profiles for a broad range of professionals as well as an expanding directory of mentors and work experience opportunities.

- Websites of employers in the field: for information about what you could do after university and what courses they like people to have done.

- Online student forums: but beware that a lot of people don't actually know the facts!

- Friends and family: although they may not be familiar with the current application process and entry requirements.

- Teachers and careers advisors: depending on their level of experience.

- People you know who have experience in that field: the best source to find out the details of any given career and also what life is really like in that career.

- University admissions tutors: the best place to find out answers to specific questions about admissions to their course that aren't already mentioned in the prospectus. They may be busy so don't worry if there is a delay in them responding to your emails.

Managing your money

With £9000 fees every year and rising costs of living, going to university costs more now than ever before. Being financially savvy will make things more comfortable for you in the long term. It's important for you to look realistically at how much your chosen degree will cost, how much debt you'll be left with and how you intend to pay that off. People now tend to study courses that lead to well-paid careers rather than studying things they are genuinely interested in. This is an unfortunate reality but there's always a way to get what you want from university. Our key tips regarding finances are:

1. Plan ahead. Budget as best you can.

2. If you work before or during university try your best to save or invest a little. Even a few pounds every month could turn into a good chunk of cash when you graduate.

3. Check out what student loan, grants or sponsorship you can get. Full details of grants can be found on the UCAS website. All the details about student loans and grants can also be found on the student finance websites (Student Finance England, Student Finance Wales, Student Finance Northern Ireland, Student Awards Agency for Scotland)

4. Keep your head above, rather than buried in the ground. It's better to look at your bank statements and see where you can improve rather than being scared to look at them and pretending it will all go away!

International applicants

Every year thousands of students from outside of the UK apply to study at UK universities. Many UK universities sit high in global university league tables and are seen as extremely prestigious, but a UK education at any university is also considered with high regard around the world. All of the advice that follows in this book applies to all applicants regardless of location, but there are a few extra things that need to be taken into consideration by international applicants. These include grade eligibility, visa arrangements, IELTS certification, moving to the UK, accommodation, personal statement writing and many other factors.

Here are some useful links providing information and support for international applicants:

UCAS:

www.ucas.com/how-it-all-works/international

Education UK:

www.educationuk.org/global

Student visa applications: https://www.gov.uk/browse/visas-immigration/study-visas

PersonalStatementChecker.com online services are perfect for international applicants, particularly those for whom English is a second language.

UCAS

The University and Colleges Application Service (UCAS) is an organisation with a central application system for most undergraduate courses and some other courses at British universities. Their website www.ucas.com has a wealth of information on how to apply and important things to think about along the way. We aren't going to repeat all of that information here but we think you'll find it useful to have this approximate timeline to help give you an overview of the whole process.

UCAS timeline

Date	UCAS deadline	What we think you should be doing
June-August		Visit your local UCAS fair Make decisions about what to apply for Finish off your work experience Create a first draft of your personal statement
September	Applications open	
October		Submit your finished application
Mid-October	Deadline for Medicine, Dentistry, Veterinary Medicine and Oxford/Cambridge	
October-November		Preparing for any aptitude tests or entrance exams
December-March		Interviews—plan ahead if you are likely to be interviewed
Mid-January	Deadline for the majority of courses	
February	UCAS Extra opens	

Late March	Deadline for some art and design courses	
March-May		Revise for your exams
Early May	Deadline to reply to all offers received before 31st March except UCAS Extra	
May-July	Several deadlines for offers received after March including UCAS Extra	
July-August		Relax; you've done the hard work!
Early August		Revisit your Plan B, and plan exactly what you will do on results day if you don't get the grades you need
Mid-August	Results day. Clearing vacancy search opens	Most Clearing vacancies are taken up very quickly in August so be quick
30th September	Final deadline for applications	Almost all of the vacancies are usually taken up well before this point

Decisions, decisions

What career?

A lot of people go to university, do a 3 year undergraduate degree and then have no idea where to go from there. For some people it can genuinely be very difficult to come to a conclusion about what the right career is for them. Indeed, a lot of people switch careers several times in their lives. There is nothing wrong with this, however, for most people, an hour or two of research while aged 17-18 can make things much clearer a few years down the line.

If you know what your ideal career is, think about what makes that career the best for you? You will always need a Plan B, so try to find an alternative that still has what attracts you to your ideal career. If you don't know what career you want, think about what you want from life or from a job. Think about which of the following you'd want from your top job.

- Work involving a subject or field you are interested in
- Meet new people
- Earn lots of money
- Use numbers/maths
- Use written English
- Care for others
- Help people through difficult times in life
- Work in a team
- Work independently

- Be creative
- Travel / Working in lots of different places
- Drive
- Graphic design and advanced IT tasks
- Opportunities for career progression
- Become an expert in one thing
- Physically active jobs
- Study for professional qualifications and to keep on learning
- Work on challenging projects
- Work at flexible times / manage your work around other commitments such as children
- Earn enough money to be comfortable but not necessarily mega-rich
- Have a routine
- Conduct research
- Manage others
- Teach others

Now that you have an idea of what you're looking for, use your sources of information (SOI) to find out which careers match what you have written. Once you've done this you will have a shortlist. Having a shortlist of potential career options before you apply for university provides you with a goal and will make the whole process a lot more streamlined and less complicated for you.

It's good to also remember that things change. What you want from a career now may be different to what you want in three years' time, and that's ok. It is still ok to plan for the future now, so long as we know that unexpected things can happen. Also, some people might do all the research that they could possibly do and still find it difficult to choose between certain careers and that is still fine. No problem.

You might not want to think about a career for now but just want to study a subject at university that you are interested in. That is totally fine and your passion for the subject should easily come across in your personal statement and give you a good chance at winning a place on your chosen course.

How to get there

Now that you have either a shortlist of potential careers or one or two broader fields of study that you find interesting, the time has come to figure out how to get there.

A-------------→***magic happens***-------------→B

For each of your ideas, look at the website for employers or organisations in that field. They may tell you what they require from applicants. Again you can use your sources to find out this information. Once you have this information, it might be helpful to write it down so you have something to refer to and something to aim for later.

For example, if you wanted to become an investment banker, employers will usually look for someone who ticks most of these boxes:

- [ ] Graduate with a 2:1 or 1st in a relevant subject such as economics or maths ideally from a high achieving university
- [ ] Passion for the subject
- [ ] Good with numbers and data processing
- [ ] Hard worker
- [ ] Team player
- [ ] Good at negotiation
- [ ] Good at coping with stress
- [ ] Professional manner of speech, written communication, dress and attitude
- [ ] Broad range of other skills and wider experiences
- [ ] Goal-oriented

Making a career plan

Now you have an idea of where you want to get to, and how to get there, it's time to make a plan. To help you with this, we've made a list of questions. The more of these you can answer, the more detailed your plan will be, so you'll be better prepared for your future. If you can't answer a question, that's ok but consider doing some more research on it.

University and course choices. What courses do people study at University in order to get into the career you want?

Experience. What work experience will you need to get into your chosen course and career?

Personal statement. What do admissions tutors for the courses you are applying to look for in the personal statement?

UCAS application. What subjects, grades or predicted grades do these courses need?

Interviews and special exams. Do the courses you are applying to require applicants to sit any special exams or go through an interview process? If so, how can you prepare for that?

Getting experience while at University. Once you're in university, what else do you need to do in order to be more employable than other graduates and beat the competition for your dream job?

Job applications. What is the best route into your dream career? Which jobs should you apply for first?

Post-graduate courses. After you've graduated, are there any special qualifications you'll need or will you need to study another degree course?

What course?

You may be surprised to know that no two university courses are the same. Each university will offer their own version of a course that may differ in content, assessment, length and/or teaching style. But don't let this overwhelm you; below you will find our easy to understand breakdown of what this all means:

Course content

A module is simply a short course of lectures, classes and seminars that you attend and will be tested on at the end of the year. Each University course is made up of modules that are compulsory and others that are optional. Use the university website, prospectus and UCAS website to help you identify the modules that make up the courses that you are interested in.

For example: An undergraduate degree in psychology at one university may consist of modules in forensic psychology and educational psychology. If these modules interest you then perhaps this course may become one of the five you apply to. However, if you are not interested in these modules and would prefer learning about social psychology, then consider narrowing your search for courses that include this module.

Course structure

Most Universities offer a three-year degree programme in which you study at University for three years and sit exams at the end of each year.

Others offer a four-year sandwich course. This means that after two years of study, you will spend one year gaining relevant work experience, after which you will go back to university and complete your final year. Many students opt for this type of course if it is available because it gives them an opportunity to develop the skills and experience they need for the workplace.

Some universities offer a three-year course with the option of a one year master's degree following completion. This four-year course does not provide students with any relevant work experience but does help them stand out from the crowd as they will have achieved a master's level qualification.

Course assessment

Each course will use its own method of assessment. Some courses will assess students using written exams that take place at the end of each year, whilst others use a combination of exams and coursework. The coursework may consist of a dissertation, lab work or mini assignments that need to be completed throughout the year.

Course learning style

Most courses are taught using a combination of lectures and small group classes however some courses offer alternative ways of learning. For example: some courses involve practical work, one to one tutorials or peer-to-peer learning (also known as problem-based learning).

At some Universities you may have to attend lots of compulsory lectures whereas the same course at another university may require you to attend a small number of lectures but have lots of independent study.

For example, medicine and dentistry schools have traditionally used lecture-based learning however approximately half of the schools in the UK now teach via problem-based learning, which you should read about in their prospectuses if this applies to you. These two styles of teaching and learning suit different types of people, and you may feel more comfortable with one style rather than the other.

Consequently, the learning style may influence your decision about which course you wish to apply to.

Accredited courses

If you have a specific career in mind, then make sure that your degree is accredited by the governing body of that profession. For example, if you want to work in the field of Psychology, then make sure that your degree is accredited by the British Psychological Society. This information is sometimes written in university prospectuses, however the website of the governing body is likely to provide you with a list of all the accredited courses.

Academic requirements and predicted grades

Each university course will provide you with the minimum academic requirements needed to get on the course. Be aware the that requirements really are a minimum and even if you meet them, the university may still refuse you a place if there are a lot of other applicants with higher grades, more experience or a better personal statement. Therefore it is important to revise early for exams, gain relevant work experience as soon as possible and produce an excellent personal statement. Personalstatementchecker.com can help advise you on relevant work experience and help you produce the best personal statement possible.

Be realistic about the grades you think you will achieve and the predicted grades your teachers will assign to you. Universities will look at predicted grades, AS grades if you declare them and sometimes even GCSEs for the more competitive courses. Therefore, don't apply to a course with high academic requirements when the grades you have achieved or your predicted grades suggest that you might not meet the academic requirements. The reverse is also true; don't apply for courses with grade requirements that are a lot lower than that which you are achieving; aim high but be realistic.

If you have achieved low Bs or lower at AS level, it is very unlikely that you will be able to resit enough to get these grades to A or A*, as well as get As in your A2 level modules (which are usually much harder). Teachers can only predict grades based on your past AS level performance and the maximum they are allowed to increase your predicted grade is usually half or one grade. For example:

AS level Maths

Grade achieved: mid-C

Likely A2 prediction: C

If you have achieved a few higher grades in class work: B or C prediction

If you have consistently achieved B-A in the classroom: B prediction

Work experience and other requirements

It is important to gain relevant work experience as soon as possible if it is required for your course. It will provide you with a realistic insight into your field of study so you'll have a better idea of whether this is the right choice for you.

Doing work experience demonstrates to admissions tutors that you are a conscientious student who has been pro-active in gaining an insight into a profession that you are genuinely interested in. It will also help you develop the professional skills that tutors are looking for. Work experience is likely to provide you with a competitive advantage against other students with similar academic achievements. Some competitive courses such as medicine require all applicants to have undertaken some relevant experience and write this in their personal statements.

Work experience can also provide you an opportunity to network and gain contact with professionals in the field who you can ask for advice at a later date.

The best time to get this experience is the summer between your AS exams and the beginning of the A2 course. The best way of getting relevant work experience is to write, email or call the person or organisation you want experience with. Your school might be able to organise some experience, but for competitive courses you'll need to be pro-active and arrange it yourself. If you get stuck, look back at the sources of information (SOI) earlier in this book for help. Admissions tutors will give you extra points if you can show that you arranged this work experience yourself as it shows a more focussed and determined attitude.

Some universities also require you to complete admissions tests such as the UKCAT for medicine or the LNAT for law. The university course webpage will list the tests you need to sit and each test will have preparation information available online.

Many courses including art and design or computer programming may require you to submit a portfolio of your work or attend a portfolio viewing session.

Which university?

There are lots of factors that will influence which universities you apply to. These include:

- Entry requirements
- Admissions process such as whether they do interviews or any special entrance exams

- Cost of living or accommodation

- Local amenities and things to do

- The course or modules on offer

As with all the other decisions we've made so far, it's best to write a list of the potential universities and use your own research and sources of information (SOI) to eliminate them until you get a nice shortlist.

Make a shortlist

Now is the time to write a list of the subject(s) you intend to study at University. You may have narrowed this down to one course, e.g. Law, or to a field of courses e.g. business with a second subject. It's useful at this stage to think about a back-up course. What would you do if you do not get into your chosen course? This is particularly important for the more competitive courses.

Your application

The Personal Statement

Overview

As undergraduate courses become increasingly competitive, the personal statement is becoming the single most important part of the UCAS application. Countless applicants will achieve the required grades, but your personal statement is what makes you stand out.

This is often your only chance to show admissions tutors who you really are and emphasise:

- Your skills and talents
- Your experience and achievements
- Your passion for the subject
- Your long term goals
- Your source of motivation

Many applicants underestimate the value of the personal statement and don't give it enough thought. A well-written personal statement is crucial for a successful application. You must do everything you possibly can to make yours stand out.

What they are looking for

The personal statement is your chance to present yourself in the best possible light in order to compel admissions tutors to give you a place.

Many admissions tutors use a numerical mark scheme to score each personal statement in the context of the whole application based on highly specific criteria.

These can vary greatly between courses, and even between admissions departments for the same course at different universities. For example, some may use a system with 6 criteria, each weighted differently with a total score of 20. Applicants who get 15 and above may get invited for an interview, those with less than 15 will not.

Some admissions tutors have found that this is the fairest way to make the admissions process as objective as possible, thereby reducing variability of assessment between readers and overall bias.

In addition to specific criteria there are certain simple features that all admissions tutors are looking for in a personal statement:

- Clear concise use of the English language without repetition or unnecessary complicated words
- An efficient structure using distinct paragraphs
- Short sentences
- Your reasons for applying to this course
- Relevant experience
- Your extracurricular activities and interests

Admissions tutors can read hundreds of personal statements each day and it can be very frustrating to read a statement that lacks the elements listed above. These are the absolute basic requirements for every personal statement; without them you simply will not be considered. Every sentence you write should convey a point. Every sentence you write should earn you a point in the admissions tutor's mark-scheme.

Another thing that admissions tutors will be looking for is your individuality. You are unique: this should be evident in your writing. Many applicants feel they need to conform to a preconceived idea of a "perfect candidate". They adopt an overtly academic approach using complex words to feign an impression of intelligence. This is the reason why personal statements are often bland, unoriginal and impersonal.

Remember, admissions tutors want to know about YOU. They are already experts in their academic field, but they know nothing about YOU. The entire purpose of a personal statement is to try and convey yourself in the most positive way within 4000 characters. You should bear this in mind and make sure that your statement really reflects your individual interests and passion.

Do's and Don'ts for UCAS Personal Statements

Do's

- Do your research and use your Sources of Information (SOI)
- Tell them WHY you are applying for this course
- Tell them what makes you a good candidate for this course
- Sell yourself
- Write using your own words
- Be as specific as possible; these details are what make your personal statement stand out from the others
- Write about YOU rather than about how good the subject is
- Be proud of your achievements but show a willingness to learn, thereby demonstrating some humility.
- Back up what you say with evidence from your reading, work experience or extra-curricular experience
- Link your points to the course you are applying to
- Be honest

- Use as much as possible of the 4000 character limit and 47 line limit
- Adhere to clear structure using paragraphs
- Talk briefly about your hobbies and interests but only if this reveals information about your suitability for this course
- Show your personal statement to a few trusted people and experts for analysis, critique and proof-reading
- Talk about your medium-term and long-term career plans if you have any
- Reflect, evaluate and offer your own viewpoint on things that other candidates might mention in order to make your statement unique. For example, many people applying to economics or finance degrees might talk about the recent financial downturn, and applicants to English degrees might mention a particular book on their A level syllabus. If you just mention this, you will not stand out from the crowd. It is your own reflection and opinion on that topic that provides evidence of originality and depth of thought.
- Start today by writing a few bullet points if you haven't already

Don'ts

- Don't lie
- Don't use humour or gimmicks. It might be funny when you read it, but admissions tutors all have different personalities and might not recognise the humour.
- Don't make arrogant claims about your greatness, especially without any evidence or examples to back it up. Admissions tutors could think you are lying if you say "I have excellent communication skills" unless you describe an experience you had which demonstrates your use of good communication skills.
- Don't copy from personal statement examples online. UCAS Copycatch similarity detection software has a database of

thousands of previous personal statements including those found online and plagiarism is taken very seriously by universities.
- Don't use services online which offer to write an entire personal statement for you based on notes you provide. It should be personal to you, in your own words.
- Don't write anything that you are not prepared to talk about in an interview
- Don't list the subjects you are studying or books you have read without explaining how this is relevant to your application
- Don't use complicated 'fancy' words
- Think twice before talking about a childhood experience. It is tempting to write something like this in the introduction "When I was 6 I visited an aquarium and since then I have been determined to become a marine biologist" or "From a young age I have always been interested in . . ." However, admissions tutors are much more interested in something more recent or what your current reasons for applying are. Saying you have "always been interested in this subject since I was a child" is surprisingly common.
- Don't mention universities by name if you are applying to more than one
- Don't rely on spell-check. Read it over and over and get others to read it for you.
- Don't spend days trying to write the opening or closing sentence. Focus more on the main content and come back later.
- Don't use a famous quote, because it's likely that many other applicants will use that quote and therefore it becomes common and loses originality. Using quotes is generally not advised because admissions tutors are more interested in what YOU have to say, rather than the words of someone else. The only exception to this would be where a particular quote has genuinely been a central and important factor in your application and has a deep relevance to the subject you are applying to.
- Don't post your personal statement online or share it with more than a few people. In particular, don't show it to people who are

applying at the same time as you. They might not want to copy you but your wording and sentence structure might get stuck in their minds subconsciously.

Section 1: introduction

Your introduction is the most important part of your personal statement. Studies on memory have demonstrated the effect of "primacy" and "recency" which refers to the fact that we are most likely to remember the beginning and the end of something such as a piece of writing. Therefore, it is important to catch their attention within the first few lines.

It is important to communicate:

- Why you want to study this course
- What makes you a suitable candidate

This can be done in many ways; however, the best statements always use evidence to back up any claim made.

For example, note the difference in these two introductions:

"I have always wanted to study Medicine because I have always had a passion for this subject. I have all the necessary skills and experience to make a good medical student."

This gives no information about who you are, what makes you unique or any detailed reason for applying to this course.

"Shadowing an A+E doctor on call in a busy inner-city hospital was the most exhilarating experience I have ever had. It was tiring but intensely rewarding and I was inspired by the doctor's diagnostic, communication and leadership skills. His rapid diagnosis saved the life of someone with a heart attack. This was the moment that I knew I wanted to become a doctor and I have been determined to achieve this goal ever since."

This immediately shows that you have had first-hand experience in the field. It demonstrates that you are goal-driven and are aware of certain skills which will benefit you in your future career. Admissions tutors now know your reason for applying to the course and it gives the impression that you will be a successful student. The last sentence also serves as a link to the next section where you will give more information about your work experience.

Another way of writing an introduction is to use an example of a particular person or event that has inspired you to pursue the subject you are applying to study. These are often very successful as they are immediately different to 80% of all other personal statements. They are also individual and unique; this is what grabs the reader's attention.

For most people, there isn't a defining moment or particular person that inspired them to study their chosen course. If you are still finding it difficult to write an introduction, think about your reasons for studying the course and write them down honestly. Applicants often feel their introduction isn't "impressive enough" but honesty is often recognised by admissions tutors and an honest introduction explaining your specific reasons for applying to the course is always a good start to a personal statement.

Whatever approach you decide to take, be sure to clearly convey your main reasons for applying to the course and give an indication that you will be a strong candidate.

Section 2: experience that makes you the ideal candidate

What you write after the introduction depends entirely on what type of course you are applying for. For some more-practical courses such as Medicine, Pharmacy, Teaching, Social Work, and some types of Engineering, work experience is very important. For more academic courses such as English, Anthropology, Psychology and Economics, work experience is not as important as showing you have a passion for the subject content. You can display this in many ways, for example wider reading and exploration. Before you read on, have a look at the relevant university's website for the course you are applying for and see whether they are most interested in work experience or academic experience (wider reading).

Regardless of what you write about, you should aim to write about what makes you the ideal applicant for this course. Every point you make should be justified with evidence from your experience.

Work experience

Work experience means any shadowing placements, work placements, part time jobs or even volunteering experiences that you have done. However they must be relevant to your application. It is usually best to start off describing the experience you have gained and use examples to justify the skills you have developed that make you a good candidate. However, do not be afraid to break this mould. If you have a unique and original way of presenting yourself, go for it. Admissions tutors enjoy reading innovative statements.

For each experience, you should consider writing about these questions:

- What was your role?
- What skills did you develop?
- What did you learn?
- How does this fit with your long-term career plan (if applicable)?
- Is there anything unique or interesting to mention?

Try to be as specific as possible when discussing your work experience. For example, every dental applicant will have done work experience with a dentist and will have learnt about the communication skills needed. So if you just write this, you will not stand out from the crowd. It is much better to try and write about something more specific such as a particular interaction with a patient and what you gained from that. It is also good to say if you organised the work experience yourself as this shows good organisation skills and motivation.

Subjects studied in school

For most courses, you should talk about any of your previous studies which are relevant to the degree you want to take. You should focus specifically on what areas of the field you are particularly interested in and any skills you have gained from these studies which you can translate to a university learning environment. It is a good idea to look at a detailed breakdown of the modules in the course you are applying for. This will allow you to identify any particular areas that you may have already covered in your previous studies or are particularly interested in studying in future, enabling you to demonstrate this knowledge and passion in your statement.

Obviously some of your school subjects will be more relevant to your future degree course than others e.g. you will definitely need to mention your English A Level studies if you are applying for a degree in English Literature. However, you may be able to demonstrate skills in your less obviously relevant studies which will still be useful e.g. in a History A Level course you will have written a lot of essays and analysed sources which will benefit you in an English Literature degree, as you will be required to write a lot of essays and analyse texts and critical sources. That said, make sure that you focus on the most relevant aspects of your previous academic experience and only mention the less relevant aspects in passing.

Wider reading

Evidence of wider reading and self-study is essential for some courses such as English, Foreign Languages or Economics. As always, it is important to be specific and also think about what will set you apart from other candidates. For example, a large proportion of Economics applicants will say they have read a book like 'Freakonomics', 'The Undercover Economist' or 'The Economic Naturalist'. However someone with a genuine understanding of what economics involves will be able to relate what they have read in these books to real life situations. For any course, it is important not to just state what you have read but to show a deeper understanding and evidence of original thought and evaluation. You could say what you learned from them and possibly express an opinion on the theories or views the writer puts forward. This engagement will show admissions tutors that you have the initiative and independent thought to be able to thrive at university level.

Section 3: broader experience

The best place to include extra-curricular activities and achievements is usually before the conclusion. However you may want to change this if, for example, being captain of your school netball team inspired you to apply for a degree in management and helped you develop leadership and interpersonal skills. Admissions tutors want to know about you as a person and extracurricular activities are an integral part of this.

Any sports or musical instruments you play, clubs you are part of, travelling, volunteering or paid work you have done (that isn't directly relevant to your course) will show admissions tutors that you are a motivated, well-rounded individual who can adapt and contribute to all aspects of university life. Again, try to focus on what skills you have gained which might be relevant to studying at university or to the course. You should use the questions listed in the previous section as prompts. This is also a good place to discuss what you intend to do on your gap year if applicable.

Some people say you should spend about 15% of your personal statement (600 characters) on the extracurricular section but different courses and departments vary in how much of this information they would like to know. Therefore it is important to look on their websites for information. If you are still in doubt, consider asking admissions tutors directly.

Section 4: conclusion

The main focus of a conclusion is to give a convincing, logical argument for admissions tutors to give you an offer. There must be a sense of finality. This is the wrong place to raise any new points about why you want to study the course you are applying for or why you would be a good candidate; these should be established earlier in your statement and only summarised in your conclusion as a reminder.

Personal statements that are written in chronological order often flow very well. Therefore, the conclusion can be a good place to mention your future plans and goals. Also, if you have mentioned any source of inspiration or motivation in the personal statement, it works well to refer to that again in the conclusion.

Every conclusion is different and must be considered in the context of the individual personal statement. Remember that your conclusion will be the last chance you have to make a lasting impression on the admissions tutor.

How to begin writing it

A blank page can be very intimidating. Here are a few simple points to get you started.

The best personal statements have been drafted and re-drafted over and over again. Admissions tutors can tell immediately if a personal statement has been rushed, so give yourself plenty of time.

Don't expect it to be perfect first time. Don't even expect it to be in full sentences. At PersonalStatementChecker.com we know most people spend longer than expected before actually starting to write their personal statements. That's why we send a writing guide to our online customers and we've included a few key tips here for you. Follow these points to start writing an excellent personal statement.

Step 1: Do your research

Look at the various universities' websites for the courses you are applying to and see if they state what they are looking for in a personal statement. Write these down.

Step 2: List anything that you could possibly write about

Focus on content by using bullet points and don't worry about grammar or sentence structure for now. Here are some ideas:

- Why do you want to study this course? Reasons could include academic interests, personal or work experience, career plans or anything else that is relevant for you.
- Why do you want to study at University?
- What experience and skills do you have that make you a good candidate?

- What have you done to prepare yourself for the course/ for studying at University?
- What are your long-term goals?
- What extra-curricular activities, experience and achievements do you have? This can include volunteering, part-time work, work experience, sports, music, awards you have won, responsibilities you hold in and out of school, travel, wider reading and any other hobbies or interests.

Don't be too selective at this stage. Just write anything and everything that comes to mind and get those creative juices flowing. You will refine this list in the next step. For now, write as much as you can.

Try to be as specific as you can; having unique answers to these questions usually leads to a great personal statement as it shows you really know what you are talking about and makes you stand out.

If you have completed any work experience, volunteered or have been employed, these are good to mention in your personal statement. You will be able to display your self-motivation, unique experience and the skills you gained from it.

If you lack experience, try to focus on your passion and ability in the subject. However, for the more competitive courses such as Medicine and Law at top universities, relevant work experience is **essential**.

Show them who you are. Break the mould. If there is someone who has inspired you, write about them. If a unique event in your life has led to your degree choice, write about it. This is what will make your personal statement **stand out** from the rest.

Step 3: Structure your points into a personal statement

Now that you have a set of notes it is time to transform this into your first draft statement. Every good statement has paragraphs, usually as listed below. It has a natural flow that makes it captivating, easy to read and well suited to the target audience; admissions tutors.

Write the following headings on a piece of paper and copy and paste your bullet points to the relevant section.

INTRODUCTION

WORK EXPERIENCE

ACADEMIC EXPERIENCE

WIDER EXPERIENCE

CONCLUSION

You might find that some points could go in both the introduction and the conclusion. Put them in one place for now, you can reconfigure them later. Once you have arranged your points into this structure take away the bullet points and headings and modify the wording. Then you should have a readable and comprehensive first draft of your personal statement.

Tip: Write a few different options for each section and keep your old versions on your computer so you can go back and re-insert something you had previously taken out.

Step 4: Flow and Evaluation

Read your personal statement again and again. Think about how the points flow together and try to use some words to connect points where appropriate. Try moving your points into different orders, or even between different sections until you are happy with it.

Evaluate your personal statement by seeing whether it meets the criteria you found out in step 1. See whether your personal statement adheres to the do's and don'ts written earlier.

Once your personal statement is at this stage it is a good idea to start showing it to a few trusted people who you know will give good advice including teachers, family and PersonalStatementChecker.com advisors. Be aware that teachers might over-emphasise the importance of your A level subjects or in-school activities. This happens because they are approaching your personal statement from a school environment. Nevertheless, they are still a good source of advice and personal statement analysis.

How to sell yourself

Everything you write in your personal statement should present you in the best light possible. Once you have outlined your basic information, experience and skills, you will need to ensure that you come across professionally. This means that your grammar and spelling should be impeccable, but it does not mean that you need to use jargon or overly fancy words. The most important thing is that your message is clear and the statement flows well.

Show off the skills you have but ensure that each skill you discuss is backed up with evidence. You could show evidence of how you developed that skill or an experience where you used that skill.

It is more impressive to show your use of a skill than to simply state you have that skill. It is also better to explain your skills in more specific terms rather than generalised skill groups. Read these two examples;

"I have great teamwork skills and I am a natural-born leader. The evidence for this is that I led my Young Enterprise company that sold handmade bracelets to the regional final, and I also gained a Duke of

Edinburgh bronze award. I have always naturally become the leader of any group I am in and I am always successful."—319 characters

"As team-leader for a Young Enterprise company, it was challenging to resolve differences of opinion in team meetings and ensure that everyone's views were heard. This experience, in addition to a Duke of Edinburgh expedition where I was responsible for navigation has developed my teamwork and leadership skills."—312 characters

The first example would probably be 'just ok' if the wild, unsupported claims at the start and end were cut out. However the second example is far better because it explains the specific details of how the applicant developed teamwork and leadership skills from these two experiences. The first example misses out this critical step.

Writing about two or three experiences or points in detail is generally better than writing briefly about six or seven different things.

How to refine it

As mentioned before, you are unlikely to get things perfect in the first draft of your personal statement; you will need to revise and refine it to make sure it is the best it can be. When you are happy with the content of your statement, you should consider improving the style and structure of the statement, which are just as important in terms of making an impact on admissions tutors.

Balancing is often overlooked but can make the difference between a good and a flawless personal statement. Ideally, every section of your statement should be equally developed and strong so that your application is well-rounded.

Here are some simple tips to help you start balancing your statement:

- Write a list of all the points you want to make and experiment with ordering them in different ways.
- Write a list of all the adjectives you want to use and experiment using them with different points, trying not to use the same word more than twice.
- Write a list of all the skills you want to show and ensure these are supported by evidence.

A logical progression from point to point is important. It is usually better to describe the most relevant points in detail first and briefly mention other less-relevant points later.

These tips just scratch the surface. After writing and revising your personal statement several times you may find it hard to spot any weaknesses and would benefit from letting someone else look at it. We highly recommend that you submit it to PersonalStatementChecker.com and use our popular online packages to refine and polish it to the highest standard possible before you send it off.

Our editors will analyse your statement in much more depth. After reading thousands of statements, they are excellent at balancing; they understand that certain points are better suited to specific parts of a personal statement and will be able to ensure that everything flows from one section to the next. They will show you how to use different sentence structures to enable you to fit more points within the character limit and make subtle changes to the emphasis of words within sentences. They will advise you about repetition of vocabulary, use of the word "I", and any other concerns you may have.

Getting your personal statement right is the key to having a successful university application. The advice and tips in this book should provide you with the tools to make a great start on writing a good statement, but if you don't want to take a risk on your future, ensure you visit PersonalStatementChecker.com and give your application an expert finish.

Interviews

Universities use interviews in different ways during the selection procedure. For some courses, an interview is an integral part of their selection procedure for all candidates. However, some departments will only interview borderline candidates and some departments will not interview any applicants. Oxford and Cambridge universities interview applicants for all of their courses and UCL and Imperial College London and other similar universities will also interview most applicants.

Professional training courses such as Medicine, Dentistry and Education are most likely to require an interview. Humanities and social science courses such as History, Geography, Foreign Languages and English are least likely to require interviews. However, there are exceptions to these so you should find out from the websites of the courses you are applying to.

If you get invited for interview don't panic! This means that the rest of your application is good enough for them to consider giving you an offer. This is a good sign. Overall, interviewers want to see genuine interest in the subject topic and a person who is capable of confident, independent thought and explanation. They are not there to 'trip you up'; they want you to show them your knowledge and skills.

Interviews come in many different shapes and sizes. Some departments will ask for a portfolio of your work, some will include written essays or tests on the day and there may even be group interview stages. The course website and admissions tutors are the best source of information and you should ensure you are clear about the format of the interview when you start preparing for it.

Preparation

- **Relax.** It is easy to get anxious about an upcoming interview. Stay positive and approach this as an opportunity to show off your enthusiasm, knowledge and skills.
- **Get the practicalities done.** Find out what the interview format will be and what the structure of the day will be including the times you will arrive and leave. Find out if you need to bring any paperwork or a portfolio and prepare this. Decide how you are going to get there and book any travel or accommodation that you might need.
- **Read the university's prospectus.** Pay attention to all the information about the course you are being interviewed for as well as general information about the university.
- **Go through your personal statement.** Interviewers could ask you about anything you have written so be prepared to answer questions on any part of your personal statement.
- **Prepare for special tests.** If there will be any tests on the day such as verbal problem solving, written tests or an essay, think about what could be asked of you and prepare and practise these so that you will be comfortable with the format. It is unlikely that they would ever expect anything from you that is more difficult than your current level of study.
- **Stay up to date.** Interviewers may ask you about new developments or important issues in your subject. There is no need to become obsessive but it is good to have a basic appreciation of the news and current developments that relate to your course. You could read a newspaper, website or magazine related to your subject, or pick out relevant articles in the mainstream news.
- **Practice.** Do mock-interviews with your teachers, friends and family. It is useful to practice with people you know who can give you feedback on the content of what you are saying. It is also useful to practice with people such as teachers that you don't

know so well. This will give you experience of a more realistic interview scenario and will help you get over any 'nerves' you may have.
- **Get advice.** Use your sources of information (SOI) including PersonalStatementChecker.com advisors who are more than willing to help and may even offer a professional mock-interview service in your area.
- **Prepare your answers (a little).** Try to write a few brief bullet points for the things you could say in response to some of the common questions that could be asked. However, do not plan exactly what to say or what wording you will use. Interviewers want to see people who have genuine interest and passion for the course and they don't favour applicants who give over-rehearsed answers. Be yourself. Do not plan to use fancy and complicated words that you don't normally say in 'real life'. If the words you use are not natural for you, you run the risk of not sounding genuine.

The interview day

- **Relax.** The night before the interview, give yourself a break and sleep early. When you wake up, try to stay calm and positive. Interviewers know that everyone gets nervous in interviews and will try to make you feel more comfortable.
- **Practical considerations.** Dress smartly. For men this almost invariably means a suit. For women there is a little more variation and you could wear a suit or a shirt/blouse with smart trousers/skirt. Whatever you wear, ensure you feel comfortable in it. Get your outfit ironed and ready the day before along with any paperwork or travel tickets you need.
- **Arrive early.** Also have the number for the university and for the admissions department for your course so that you can tell them if you are going to be late for an unavoidable reason.

- **Body language.** Smile, make comfortable eye contact and sit up straight. Try to avoid slouching, yawning or folding your arms.
- **Don't panic.** When they ask a question, take a few moments to think about your answer before just saying the first thing that comes to mind. Once your points have finished, summarise what you have said and then stop talking. This will help you to avoid waffling and trailing answers.
- **Listen carefully.** Listen to their questions carefully and answer what they have asked you, rather than talk about something slightly different that you may have prepared for.
- **Ask for clarification.** If you don't understand the question it is ok to ask them to repeat or rephrase it.
- **Be honest.** If you don't know the answer to a question, just say so. Interviewers don't expect you to know everything and may just be pushing you towards the limits of your knowledge.
- **Ask questions if you have any.** If you have questions, it is fine to ask your interviewers at the end of the interview and this can show enthusiasm and maturity.

Afterwards

- **Relax (for the third time!).** Don't worry if you found it difficult. Some interviewers aim to test the limits of your knowledge or skills, so you may have actually scored all the marks necessary well before the tough questions. You've done the hard work and now you can give yourself a well-deserved break.

- **Have a look around.** This could be the place you spend the next few years of your life so feel free to explore the local area if you haven't already.

- **Write notes.** Write down the questions you had and answers you gave. This could be useful for future interviews you have.

Think about which answers went well and which could be improved for the future.

- **Stay positive.** There is no benefit in worrying about the interview now as worrying will not change the outcome. Look to the future whether that is further interviews, exams or a nice break and wait for the result.

Aptitude tests

Many courses now require applicants to sit a variety of special entry exams alongside their UCAS application. These exams are all different and usually specific to the course you are applying to. Furthermore, each university may use the results of these exams differently, so there is not on universal "pass mark".

The number of exams is increasing every year, as is their complexity so here are some tips to take into consideration:

- Check the entrance exam requirements for the courses you are thinking of applying to in the university prospectus or on their website.
- Visit the website for the exam well before you apply and try out some of the sample questions to get a feel for it. You might find you are going to need a lot of preparation for it or you might even find that the topic doesn't interest you as much as you thought it might.
- Prepare as much as you can. These exams are as important as your A levels, if not more. So you should definitely invest time and effort into preparing for these. There are usually guides and example questions for you to practice with. If you get stuck on how to prepare, ask your careers advisor, the organisation that provides the exam, or students from last year.

Subject-specific advice

In this section we'll discuss each of the most popular courses or fields that people apply to and tell you everything you'll need to know in order to get in. Our team have spent time with admissions tutors and have taken part in admissions panels so we are confident that this expert knowledge will help you get a place on your first-choice degree course. For each subject we will focus on what they are looking for in your personal statement. We will also discuss important points that are specific to that subject area.

Medicine

A degree in Medicine will provide the knowledge and skills required to become a junior doctor in the UK. This includes an understanding of how the human body works in health and in illness, anatomy, pharmacology and time spent with patients in hospital and in primary health care gaining skills and experience in professional communication amongst other things. This is one of the most competitive courses offered by UK universities and is the only degree in the UK that allows you to become a doctor and gain registration with the GMC (General Medical Council), the governing authority for doctors in the UK. UCAS applications must be submitted by the October deadline and you can make a maximum of 4 choices.

A lot of people feel pressured into applying for medicine. This could be because there are other doctors in the family or there is a social or cultural status associated with being a doctor. You must remember that although other people want you to be a doctor, it will be you that has to go through the degree and it will be you that will be doing the job for the next 50 years. This affects your life more than it affects others so you must make sure that applying to medicine is YOUR decision and that you are happy with it.

Course content

There are a huge variety of approaches to teaching Medicine at UK Medical Schools but they tend to fall within these categories:

1: Pre-clinical years then clinical years. The traditional way of teaching Medicine is to spend two years in the university learning about how the body works and then spending the last few years primarily learning about health and disease with lots of patient contact on hospital wards or in primary care. The first years are taught either with modules of different disciplines such as physiology, anatomy, immunology, pharmacology, biochemistry or in terms of body systems where you would have a module on respiratory medicine where you would learn everything relating to the lungs including anatomy, physiology, pharmacology etc.

2: Early clinical experience courses. Some medical schools put much more emphasis on patient contact in the first few years and in these medical schools you may even gain patient contact and experience from the first week.

A. Primarily PBL (problem based learning). Courses taught in this way involve weekly tutorials on a particular topic such as angina, then lots of time for independent and group study around the topic and then the opportunity to present your knowledge about the topic to your peers and the tutor in the following week. PBL provides an opportunity for developing your organisational skills, team skills and comfort with independent learning. However it may come as a shock for people who are used to being told everything they need to know.

B. Primarily lectures. Some medical schools still teach using lectures primarily with much less emphasis on independent study.

All medical schools will be a configuration of the above categories, for example a course that has a clear divide between pre-clinical and clinical years and teaches using a lot of lectures will be 1B. However, in reality most medical schools are modifying their courses to include more and more patient contact and provide a variety of teaching styles and methods. There is also much more emphasis on learning the skills required to be a good doctor such as sensitive communication skills and understanding things from a patient's perspective. These skills were not taught in medical schools until relatively recently.

Competition Ratios

According to the latest figures from UCAS, on average there are 10 applications for every place in a UK medical school and this figure has remained stable for the last few years. If you think that every person can make 4 applications, there are probably 2.5 people applying for every place. Approximately 2 out of every 3 applicants will get at least 1 interview. Once you get to interview stage the competition decreases, and between 50% and 70% of those invited to interview get offers.

There is no such thing as a "good" or a "bad" medical school and the older schools in the UK are not any better than the newer schools. Getting a medical degree and GMC registration already puts you in the top few percent of ability in the general population. It does not matter which UK medical school you graduate from. The fact that you have graduated is what counts.

Academic entry requirements

The academic requirements are usually AAA at A-level and a B in a further AS level with both Chemistry and Biology at A2 or AS level. Thousands of medical applicants get these grades so many medical schools look at GCSE grades in more detail. Most medical schools also ask that A levels are completed within a two year period (i.e. they don't count the grades you achieve in any resits after year 13), and some medical schools will even look at your module scores for the first time you sat an exam for a particular module.

For IB students the criteria is usually 36-38 points as a bare minimum. You should check the websites of the medical schools you are looking at to see what their overall IB point requirement is and whether they require a specific amount of points from specific subjects.

Being realistic about your grades and predicted grades is very important for medicine. Every year we come across so many applicants who desperately want to study medicine and think that they will be able to get the grades at A2 even though they have achieved B's at AS. If you have achieved low B's or lower at AS level, it is very unlikely that you will be able to resit enough to get these grades to A or A*, as well as get A's in your A2 level modules (which are usually much harder).

UKCAT and BMAT

Almost all medical schools require you to sit an admissions test and the UKCAT is more widely used than the BMAT. Both are primarily multiple-choice exams done under very tight time conditions at test centres in the UK and abroad. They are aimed at seeing if you have the required standard of problem solving skills, professional ethical attitudes, mental abilities, reasoning abilities and other skills considered to be valuable for future doctors.

It is difficult to revise for these tests because they do not really test any science knowledge. However, it is very important to practice the questions as much as you possibly can and do this under timed conditions so that you get used to the type and style of questions, the way in which you will be asked to think, and also the extremely tight time you have in which to answer all of the questions. Situational Judgement Questions (SJQs) are a recent addition and are becoming more popular in medical schools every year. These tell you a scenario and ask you to rank the available options from the best option to the worst option of what to do in that scenario. They will be very strange if you are unfamiliar with them so our top tips are:

1. Practise practise practise

2. Read the question—subtle changes in wording can affect which options they want you to pick first.

Different medical schools use these tests in different ways. For example some medical schools will only give interviews to people who have achieved a certain UKCAT score, and some other medical schools will only use the UKCAT or BMAT score to decide between borderline candidates who have already had interviews. There is not much point in being strategic about these test**s**. The bottom line is you need to do them and you need to do them to the best of your ability.

You should be booking these tests and preparing for them during the summer before you submit your UCAS application. More information can be found on the UKCAT and BMAT websites and the websites of the medical schools will tell you which test they use.

Work experience

Work experience is essential for anyone applying to medicine but admissions tutors acknowledge how difficult it is to get relevant work experience. Admissions tutors don't necessarily look for how much work experience you have done; they are generally more interested in what you gained from that experience. When you are on work experience, you should ask lots of questions and take notes every day on what you have done and what you have learnt so that you can write this in your personal statement.

Having about 2-3 weeks of work experience is an average amount for successful applicants, but please remember that admissions tutors will value a candidate who did one week of experience but gained a lot from it, rather than a candidate who has done 10 weeks of experience but hasn't shown that they learnt anything from it.

Relevant work experience can include:

- GP surgery: aside from spending time in the reception area, try to spend time with the GPs or nurses if possible and ask them lots of questions about their jobs and the good and bad points of working in healthcare etc. There may be confidentiality issues meaning that you can't sit in with the GP while he/she sees patients, but there's still a lot you can learn from the reception. For example you could learn about how referrals are made, how waiting times are managed, and how complaints are dealt with.

- Hospitals: You can get work experience with doctors, nurses and other allied health professionals. It is all useful for your application. Call your local hospitals and try and speak to someone in the education centre who organises work experience. There are very few work experience opportunities in hospitals so don't worry if you can't do this.

- Care homes: Volunteering in a care home either for a week or two continuously or once a week for an extended period of time will give you lots of experience in caring for patients and seeing how care is given to people in need. It is usually quite easy to arrange this experience if you ask enough.

- Dentists, pharmacists, patient charity organisations e.g. Age concern, Macmillan trust, hospices: These are all places where care in given to patients in the NHS. There is a lot you can learn from these places that is relevant to medicine.

- Part-time jobs: If you have a part-time job alongside studying your A-levels this can help show that you have organisation skills and a professional attitude. If this job involves speaking with people, you have also developed a lot of interpersonal skills too. This is very relevant to medicine.

- Other long-term volunteering: Many medical schools prefer candidates who have shown a more long-term commitment (i.e. over 6 weeks) to helping people in a structured way. This could include helping at a charity shop, St John's ambulance, volunteering at a hospital or other place of care, or even looking after an elderly or disabled relative.

You get extra points if you can show that you arranged the work experience yourself because this displays genuine enthusiasm, motivation, organisation and a positive attitude towards medicine. You can write this in your personal statement or ensure that your teachers have mentioned it in your reference.

Back when I applied, I wrote 200 letters, 200 emails and made about 50 phone calls to GPs and care homes in the West Midlands. I got about 20 replies saying 'no', but I got one letter from a GP surgery offering me one week of work experience, and a call back from a nursing home offering me two weeks of volunteering experience. If you feel like you aren't getting anywhere, don't worry, just keep on going. If you contact enough places, eventually someone will offer you something. Of course you should always consult your Sources of Information (SOI) who will definitely be able to help you.

Personal Statements

The personal statement is absolutely critical for medical applications. The structure of a personal statement for medicine should usually be:

1. Introduction—why do you want to be a doctor? Summarise why you would be a good medical student or a good doctor.

2. Work experience—give a brief overview of what you did and then focus on what you learnt and how this inspired you to become a doctor.

3. Extra-curricular and other experience—focus on what skills you have developed that would be useful for a medical student or for a doctor.

4. Conclusion—There are lots of things you can write as a conclusion. Some ideas are a summary of what would make you a good medical student or doctor, or what you intend to do as a doctor.

Personal statements for medicine tend to be very similar so it's often difficult for admissions tutors to distinguish between them. Therefore, while the usual structure is listed above, don't be afraid to break the mould and write in a way that is more personal to you. After all, it is a personal statement. Also, try to be as specific as possible, because it is the specific details in your personal statement that will make it memorable and different to everyone else's.

Our editors at PersonalStatementChecker.com include several doctors from UK medical schools. We have a wealth of experience in medical schools admissions and know what admissions tutors are looking for. There is a lot more advice we can give about medical personal statements, tailored to your application and what you need. Our company director is a doctor and medicine is our specialist field so if you are applying to medicine, you should definitely seek our help.

Interviews

The format of medical school interviews varies greatly, but in essence they are all looking for the following things:

- Realistic expectation of the career demands

- Able to hold a sensible professional conversation

- Ease of communication with people you've never met before

- Genuine interest and motivation to spend your life treating patients

- Honesty

- A well-rounded personality

- Ability to cope with pressure (i.e. staying calm in the interview process)

- Ability to reason and work through difficult scenarios

Different medical schools assess applications in different ways but overall, once you are invited to interview you are more than 50% likely to get an offer. There's a lot you can do to prepare for the interview and we would recommend practice makes perfect.

Get practice questions from the internet and work through them with your friends, teachers, family, or anyone else! At the time of writing this, PersonalStatementChecker.com is developing interview preparation courses so watch this space.

Interviews don't generally test any knowledge; they are more focused at assessing the skills and characteristics listed above. However there is a certain amount of knowledge that you should have:

- What the format of interviews will be in the medical schools you are applying to.

- Information about the medical school, how their medical course is taught and about the university overall.

- A basic, background knowledge of current news relating to the NHS or medicine. You don't need to know too much detail, but it is definitely worthwhile doing some reading. We would recommend reading the health section of any mainstream news source such as a news website or mainstream newspaper. If you have access to the BMJ or studentBMJ this can be useful although it might be a little too detailed.

- A basic understanding of what happens after medical school. In the UK, all medical school graduates will gain a provisional registration with the GMC and a license to practice medicine. After medical school all graduates apply for the Foundation Training programme which lasts for 2 years; Foundation Year (FY) 1 and 2. After the first year they gain full registration with the GMC and after the second year they can enter speciality training which can be in general practice, hospital medicine, hospital surgery or a variety of other specialities such as psychiatry, obstetrics and gynaecology etc. After this stage, they become registrars and then go through further training that can last anywhere between 3 and 8 years before they become consultants or GPs.

What to do if you don't get in

If you are applying for medicine or any competitive course, it is essential to think about what your Plan B will be. Every year we come across a lot of people who really wanted to apply for medicine but don't manage to get in. There are always lots of options, so we've listed a few scenarios below.

1. You want to apply to medicine but did not get high enough GCSE or AS grades.

   It will be difficult for you to re-sit enough modules to bring your grades high enough alongside getting As in your A2 modules. It will also be difficult for your teachers to predict you enough As to get into medicine this time around. In this situation it is worth thinking about alternatives to medicine where you can still get what you want out of your career. If you want to help patients, think about nursing, physiotherapy, optometry or pharmacy for example. If you want to help people in general, think about working with the police, the fire service or care work for example. If you want a job where you will make a comfortable salary, think about accounting, finance or law. You should consider applying for biomedical sciences BSc if you enjoy studying biology or chemistry at school and this is your main reason for choosing medicine.

   Some people think about applying for biomedical sciences BSc and then applying for graduate entry medicine. This option will provide you with a degree in three year's time that will be valued in the world of work. However, very few people actually make it from biomedical sciences into medical school because the competition for graduate entry medicine is even tougher than the competition for undergraduate entry medicine. Furthermore, if you do medicine as a second degree, you will have to pay the tuition fees upfront and this might not be affordable for you.

2. You missed out slightly on either the AS grades or the admissions test results and didn't get any interviews

   If you only missed out slightly, it might be worthwhile to take an extra year to get more experience and improve your grades

Subject-specific advice

then apply again. Be aware that some medical schools may not accept applicants who have taken more than 2 years to complete their A levels so make sure you check their websites or ask their admissions tutors for clarification about whether you can apply next year. It is not worth taking this route if you missed out by a big margin because you will have too much to catch up on in a short space of time. However, in this situation it is again worthwhile reassessing what you want from your degree, from your career and from your life. Maybe there is an alternative to medicine that will still give you what you want.

3. You got the right AS grades and admissions test results but didn't get any interviews

   This is the ideal situation to take a year out to get more experience and apply again. You will have access to more work experience because you will be over 18 and you can show genuine commitment to medicine in your personal statement.

4. You got the right AS grades and admissions test results, you got an interview but no offers

   Again this is a good situation in which to reapply next year. However in this situation you should definitely contact the medical school and ask for written feedback on your interview performance. They might tell you areas of improvement which you can work on in the year out.

5. You got an offer but didn't get the right A2 level grades to meet that offer

   On results day you should call the medical school and see if they will still accept you. They might put you on a waiting list in case some people drop out in the first few weeks of the first term. Alternatively, they may offer you a deferred place for the following year but this is rare.

Dentistry

Dentistry is a vocational course that provides the knowledge, skills and experience to become a dentist in the UK.

Dentistry and Medicine are taught in very similar ways and there is considerable overlap in terms of what you are taught in the early years. Admissions for Dentistry and Medicine are also very similar and they both require broadly the same things. Therefore, anyone applying to Dentistry should read our Medicine section above. We will only write advice specific to Dentistry applications below.

Work experience

Obtaining work experience with a community dental practice is quite easy if you can contact enough places and most applicants have done this. To differentiate yourself from other applicants you need to write about what you gained from that experience in the way we have described in our personal statement chapter. You may be able to secure work experience in a dental hospital, with dental technicians or with maxillo-facial surgeons if you contact them well in advance.

As with medicine, getting broader work experience in a caring role or in a role when you constantly meet members of the public is very useful for dentistry as this will develop skills crucial for being a good dentist.

Personal statements

All the advice in the medicine section applies here but there are a few things specific to dentistry that you must think about. Dental schools want to see evidence of your manual dexterity, i.e. evidence that you are comfortable and competent at work involving intricate hand movements. This could be anything from playing a musical instrument to painting bowls of fruit or sewing. If you cannot think of anything that you do that will display this skill, think about starting to do something for example teaching yourself how to carve wood.

Showing a specific interest in an aspect of dentistry or a certain field within dentistry will help make your application unique. If you can't think of any specific field within dentistry that appeals to you, have a look at the range of dental careers available and see if you find any of them particularly interesting. However, don't pretend to have a specialist interest if you genuinely don't have one. You may instead be motivated by the ability to help people suffering with pain, or by the prospect of a stable job in uncertain economic times. Whatever your reasons for applying to dentistry, make sure you explain them clearly and succinctly in your personal statement.

Interviews

For dental school interviews, you may be asked to bring in evidence of your manual dexterity to talk about. This could be a folder portfolio of your artwork, a knitted jumper you made or anything else as discussed in the above section. You are also expected to have a basic knowledge of dentistry, such as defining fundamental dental conditions such as tooth erosion, caries, gum disease and dentine hypersensitivity. You might be asked what you understand about certain specialities in dentistry such as orthodontics, periodontics or oral surgery etc. You are not expected to know much more than a basic definition for these terms.

Nursing, Pharmacy and other health or social care degrees

"Subjects Allied to Medicine" is a hugely diverse group of vocational and non-vocational courses leading to a wide range of careers. This includes degree courses leading to qualifications that allow you to work as health and social care professionals in the UK such as Nurses, Physiotherapists, Social Workers, Pharmacists, Dental technicians and so on.

The common theme running through all of these courses and all of these careers is that they are all caring professions, aimed at improving the health and wellbeing of other people. If you want to work in a caring profession but are not sure exactly which caring profession to choose, the "subjects allied to medicine" section of the UCAS directory is a good place to start. You will be surprised at the variety of careers available, some of which you may never have heard of.

Many people want to be doctors and dentists, but they may not know that healthcare in the UK is offered by teams, and other professionals including nurses, social workers, occupational therapists and technicians all make up the multi-disciplinary team that helps patients. Most healthcare professionals working in the NHS (which is the UK's largest employer) enter the NHS pay scale, which is standardised and offers reasonably well-paid, stable employment for thousands of people.

Some of the courses in this section tend to be extremely competitive such as nursing and pharmacy. Therefore, look at the application statistics and entry requirements on the university websites so that you know what it will take to get an offer.

Entry requirements

Academic entry requirements vary greatly between these courses, but in general tend to be lower than medicine and dentistry. For all of these courses, it is useful to have some work experience in an environment specific to that course such as shadowing a pharmacist or volunteering at a nursing home. However, this is not a requirement and the vast majority of these courses will accept applicants who have demonstrated work experience in any caring profession or volunteering in a caring role. This is because the skills and knowledge you will gain from caring for people are transferable across the whole sector.

Personal Statement

The personal statement should have emphasis on work experience and evidence of skills gained from volunteering or other hobbies and activities. It is not critical to discuss your A levels unless there is something specific that relates to the course you are applying for. The structure should be the same as that for medicine and dentistry.

'People skills' are extremely important to demonstrate for personal statements in these fields. You should also demonstrate an understanding of what the career you are applying to involves. It is useful to talk about a specific interest you have due to your past experience and things you have read. However if you do this, ensure that you also show a willingness to learn about other aspects of that career. For example you may be applying to a social care degree because you have developed a passion to help children with disabilities, but ensure that you show you are willing to learn about social care in a broader sense, relating to different groups of people.

Being specific is as important as for every other degree. Saying "I like looking after babies" is not enough to win you a place on a midwifery course. Most health and social care careers are frequently in the news or have new developments and issues as they adjust to new government policy or the changing culture and make-up of UK society in the 21st century. Therefore it is important you make an effort to find out the latest news in your field. You may be asked about this at interview.

What to do if you don't get in

If you don't get in to these courses be aware that a lot of these courses offer places in UCAS Clearing. There is a very broad range of careers available in healthcare, so if you keep an open mind and look carefully enough using your sources of information, you stand a good chance of finding something you are interested in. If your academic qualifications do not meet the entry requirements but you still want to work in a caring profession, there are other careers that do not require degree-level qualifications. These include healthcare assistants, certain types of social workers and many others. These can be very rewarding and stable careers with great opportunities for career development and moving up the ladder.

Nationally there is often a shortage of professionals in certain healthcare careers. Recent shortages include nursing and audiology. Sometimes the NHS may offer a grant or subsidiary if individuals complete these courses so look around for what is available when you apply.

Law

Undergraduate degrees in law cover law and legal process in detail, with a specific focus on law in the UK. If you want a career in law as a barrister or solicitor, a degree in law is not mandatory and you can do a 1 or 2 year law conversion course after many other undergraduate degrees.

Entry requirements

Entry requirements vary from mostly Bs to straight As at A level depending on the institution and its "prestige". Be aware that getting a law degree from a "prestigious" university does not guarantee success in your career, and many people who study law at newer universities with lower grade requirements go on to become very successful in the field of law. The older law schools tend to study more Jurisprudence (the study and theory of law) and Legal History whereas newer schools tend to offer more modules where you will learn common law, statute and EU law that affect life in the UK.

LNAT, the national assessment test for law

Satisfactory performance at LNAT is a requirement at some universities including UCL, Birmingham, Durham, Bristol, Kings College London, Oxford, Nottingham and Glasgow at the time of writing. It does not test any knowledge of law and consists of a multiple choice section and a short essay question. The multiple choice section tests your ability to discriminate, analyse or summarise the evidence being presented to you. The 600-word essay question will ask you a question that could provoke different opinions, such as "Should the law require people to vote in general elections?" There is no right or wrong answer but they do expect you to come off the fence by declaring a position and defending that position. The argument you put forward should be structured clearly so you will need to think about your points before writing them down. A good answer will be structured like this;

1. Introduction

2. For

3. Against

4. Conclusion

They are assessing your ability to formulate a clear, concise and convincing argument. The test is tightly timed so it is advisable to practise as much as you can before you sit it. See their website, www.lnat.ac.uk for more information.

Personal statements

In your personal statement you should write a clear explanation of your main reasons for applying to law. You could talk about something or someone that inspired you, or something you have read in or out of school that you have reflected on from a legal dimension. You could also discuss an aspect of current affairs from a legal viewpoint.

Law schools are looking for well-rounded applicants with an interest in current affairs and a genuine, specific and unique reason for wanting to study this course. They don't necessarily favour candidates who have work experience in law firms. They favour candidates who can show that they have gained transferable skills from work experience, hobbies and other activities such as sport or music that have prepared you for the demands of a law degree. Some possible hobbies that relate well to law include public speaking and debating but anything can count as long as you demonstrate that this activity will make you a good law student. Talking about a part-time job and what you have gained from it is worthwhile as this shows skills such as maturity, responsibility and dedication.

As with other courses it is important to be specific and unique with your reasons for applying to that course. Saying you were inspired by a legal drama show on TV is not unique and will not help you stand out from the crowd. Good quality of written-language is extremely important for UCAS personal statements for law.

Economics

You might think that studying Economics might be your road to riches, and you may well be right. Economics graduates enjoy high employability and a higher-than-average income, which makes this course very competitive, especially at the more prestigious universities.

However, it is important not to lose sight of what economics actually is and what the course involves.

Economics can be defined broadly as the study of the choices we make, as individuals, groups, companies and even countries, and the factors that influence these choices. Another definition is "the study of the factors that influence income, wealth and well-being" (Quality Assurance Agency for Higher Education). It combines maths and statistics with social science and many other fields such as politics and law to analyse and critically evaluate real-world situations.

Some economics departments look for candidates with exceptionally strong quantitative skills, with Further Maths A level (or IB equivalent) being mandatory for some courses. However other departments look for candidates with breadth of experience at A level and value candidates that can demonstrate they gained something from broader subjects. Some universities do not require Maths at A level but all universities tend to have a minimum standard of at least a pass in GCSE Maths. Regardless of the requirements, maths is an integral part of most economics courses so if you have done maths, it will make the course more familiar for you.

If you are interested in economics and another field of study, you will be pleased to find that economics is often offered as a joint degree with other subjects such as maths, politics, history and several others.

Economics graduates are highly sought-after in the world of business. This is because they develop a number of skills to a very high standard such as fluency in finance and managing money, an analytical viewpoint, health scepticism about the misuse of data, and the ability to apply quantitative methods and computer techniques to solve a range of real-world problems.

The Personal Statement

Demonstrating a genuine enthusiasm for the subject and backing this up with evidence is the key to a good economics personal statement. To show this, you could talk about your wider reading including relevant books, articles, or issues in the news and current affairs. You could even talk about your own analysis of a real-world issue. When discussing books, try to show what you learnt from that book and then try to apply that knowledge to a situation that you have come across. This will make the point more specific and unique to you, as well as demonstrating you are able to analyse, evaluate and apply data.

If there is a particular field of economics that interests you, talk about it. However don't pretend to be interested in something if you know little about it. If you have medium or long-term goals it would be useful to discuss how an Economics degree will help you achieve your goals or fit in with your career plan.

Work experience and voluntary work can be mentioned briefly but ensure that everything you write is related to your interest in economics or evidence that shows you will be a good economics student at university.

Business Studies and Management

A degree in business studies provides you with a theoretical and practical understanding of how successful businesses are run. You will learn about everything from strategic marketing, recruitment and business management to consumer behaviour and economics. Business studies is a competitive course with some universities receiving 5000 applications for 500 places. Business graduates often go on to work in finance, marketing, operations and human resources. Others go on to start up their own companies. A business studies degree makes you a very desirable employee for many different roles in both public and private sector organisations.

Academic and other entry requirements

The academic requirements to study business vary considerably from AAA-CCC or 35 points at IB. Admissions tutors often look for candidates with a broad range of skills including quantitative skills gained from doing maths and science subjects as well as analytical and essay skills gained from subjects such as English or history.

If you are considering a career in business or management, it is important to show that you have a realistic expectation of the challenges of business. You can develop this through work experience, part-time jobs, activities such as Young Enterprise or even if you have set up your own business.

The personal statement

Admissions tutors for business degrees are generally more interested in the skills you have developed and your reasons for applying to this degree rather than wider reading. After your introduction it is a good idea to discuss what you have gained from work experience and other activities before talking about what you have gained from your A-levels. Talking about your A-level subjects will not differentiate you from the thousands of other applicants for this course so take time to focus on the skills you have developed from your curricular and extra-curricular activities.

Some key skills are self-motivation, an ability to work as an individual and as a team player, and good inter-personal skills. Ensure you can show evidence of these skills in your personal statement. As always, it is important to use specific examples as evidence of how and why you developed these skills. Please refer back to the personal statement section of this book for further advice.

Psychology

Psychology is the scientific study of human behaviour and is one of the most popular undergraduate degrees offered. Some of the top universities receive 1600 applications for just 110 places.

Most universities (with the exception of Oxford and Cambridge) do not ask students to sit additional tests to apply for a psychology degree, however some universities ask students to submit an essay or complete a research task which they must send to the admissions tutor. Students are often asked to do this by the university at the interview or a letter is sent to them with clear instructions about what they are expected to do.

Career destinations

A psychology degree provides students with a broad range of transferable skills such as the ability to conduct and write up research, analyse and critically evaluate information as well as an ability to work independently and as part of a group. Consequently, Psychology graduates go on to work in a variety of professions including human resources, banking, teaching, research, further study and jobs in psychology including clinical, education, forensic, health and sports psychology.

Academic and other entry requirements

The academic requirements for undergraduate degree in psychology vary from A*AA-DDC depending on the university you apply to. Some universities state that they would like you to have studied at least one science or maths based subject at A level.

Work experience is not essential because it is quite difficult to find work experience in psychology due to the confidential and sensitive nature of the job. However, you can use the British Psychological Society website to find the names and contact details of professionals to arrange work experience with including educational, sports, health or forensic psychologists. As with most degree choices, completing voluntary work or working part time shows admission tutors that you are a responsible, mature and organised individual who can manage the work load of a degree based course.

The personal statement and interviews

Admissions tutors want to know:

- Why you are applying to study psychology. Candidates who show a genuine and deep interest will be favoured by admissions tutors.

- What have you done to explore the study of psychology outside of school or in other subjects? For example, have you read any relevant books, articles or news stories? Ensure you mention these within your personal statement. This will help prove your genuine interest in psychology and that you are capable of independent work, which is useful as most psychology degrees involve a lot of self-learning and independent study time.

- Any fields of psychology that you are interested in and why.

- What you intend to do after studying this degree.

- What makes you well prepared for studying a degree in general? Talk about any work experience, jobs, extra-curricular or other activities that you have done which show you have the skills necessary to do well at university.

Engineering

Engineering is about creation, applying scientific, economic, social and practical knowledge to design, build, improve or maintain structures, machines, devices, systems, materials and processes. It is a hugely varied field of study with a broad range of career outcomes. There are a lot of available 'sandwich courses' that include a year in industry where you work in a company and (usually) get paid for one year in between the second and third years of your university degree. Degrees are accredited by the Engineering Council (UK) and their website www.engc.org.uk is a useful source of information for anyone applying to engineering. If you have a creative personality, you stand a good chance at finding a field of engineering that appeals to you. Have a look through www.tomorrowsengineers.org.uk or www.theiet.org for information about different fields of engineering and things you can do to find out more.

Academic and other entry requirements

Academic entry requirements vary greatly and many courses require applicants to have completed specific subjects at GCSE or A level, (or equivalent) usually including mathematics. As every field of engineering involves the practical application of scientific theory, work experience and some 'real-world' experience outside of school is important. Work experience does not necessarily have to be in engineering but you should relate your work experience to the content of your chosen course in some way, or show that you have gained skills useful for your chosen course.

The personal statement

Admissions tutors are looking for candidates who can clearly explain what got them interested in engineering. Creative people who are self-motivated, original and have a passion for their subject are favoured. Think about what you have done that can show these traits.

Remember that admissions tutors are not interested in your childhood experiences, so talking about how much you loved playing with building blocks will not earn you a place at university! Showing evidence of an understanding of a particular problem and the steps needed to work towards a solution is a good idea. Engineers in all fields work in teams so team skills as well as leadership is important to demonstrate.

As most engineering degrees are specific to a discipline from the start, it is important that your entire personal statement is relevant to that particular field. However be aware that some universities offer degrees in general engineering that do not specialise until later on the course. If you are applying to these courses, ensure that your personal statement includes information that relates to a range of engineering disciplines.

Computer Science

Computer science degrees explore the foundations of computation (any calculation or use of technology that follows well-defined rules or algorithms) and information processing (using these models to manipulate and transform data into computers). Studying computer science involves a systematic approach to methodical processes to aid the acquisition, representation, processing, storage, communication of, and access to information. The applications of computer science are vast and many fields of study linked to computer science such as information technology and software engineering are at the cutting edge of human innovation and modern technology. There are a growing number of potential specialist topics you can cover on computer science degrees. These include programming, graphics, games development, interface design and advanced internet.

Academic and other entry requirements

Further maths and/or physics are required for many computer science degrees. Broader subjects such as business studies, sociology or geography could add an interesting dimension to your application as you will be better able to reflect on how humans use information. Learning a beginner programming language such as C++ or Pascal is important and some universities ask for this specifically.

The personal statement

The key to writing a good personal statement for computer science is to keep it personal and show genuine enthusiasm for the subject. Talk about any programming you have done, what you learnt from it, what you enjoyed about it and what you intend to do next. If you have an online presence or portfolio, ensure that your referee knows about it so they can include a link in the reference. This is also something you can talk about in your personal statement. Team skills and organisation skills are important in all disciplines of computer science so you should show evidence of these skills in your personal statement. A clear reason for what inspires you to study computer science is a must for any personal statement in this field.

Media and Journalism

Journalism is a very varied profession, with roles ranging from music critic to war correspondent, and it is changing rapidly thanks to digital advances. If you are considering being a journalist, you should be curious, interested in current affairs and trends and a good communicator. A degree in Journalism will provide training across a range of platforms and teach you the role of multimedia journalism today. It will develop your writing skills and ability to discover a news story, and you will learn about the latest legal and ethical developments in the industry. Teaching methods include workshop-based core skills modules, lectures by practitioners, student-led seminars and guided research. You will also be given chances to gain practical work experience. Assessment methods are based mainly on the production of news stories, features and essays.

A Media degree may be right for you if you are interested in issues relating to the production and consumption of media and cultural objects such as art, film, television, music and literature. On this course, you will look at the relationship between media, culture and society, and develop practical skills needed for this industry. You will learn to develop your critical and creative abilities through theoretical and practical studies. Teaching methods include lectures, seminars, practical workshops, presentations and tutorial support. You will also be taught important technical skills. Assessment methods are likely to include practical productions, essays, group and individual seminar presentations, study logs, a dissertation and exams. Towards the later stages of your degree, you should be able to tailor your module choices towards your interests and career goals.

Career destinations

While these degrees are will prepare you for a career in the creative sector, the critical, creative and interdisciplinary skills you will develop will enable you to work successfully in other fields.

The range of careers available in journalism is vast. Journalists work across national, regional and local newspapers, magazines of all kinds, online publications, broadcast journalism and are also sought after in other industries such as public relations, advertising and publishing. The Media industry is similarly broad, meaning you could end up working as a copywriter, a web content editor or a film-maker. There is an increasing amount of work in digital roles such as data journalist and online community manager.

Academic requirements

Usually, universities do not ask for specific A-levels from Journalism applicants. However, it is obviously useful to have studied essay-based subjects such as English as you will need to demonstrate your writing proficiency. Other relevant A-levels include History and Politics, which indicate that you have an awareness of current affairs. For Media, Media Studies or any other similar A-levels are beneficial.

Work experience

Including relevant work experience will really strengthen your personal statement as it will show that you are committed to this industry and have begun to gain the necessary skills to be successful in it. You could try to obtain a placement at a local newspaper or work on your school magazine (if you don't have one, why not try starting one yourself?). Failing that, you could look out on the internet for websites you can contribute to or make your own blog. This is fairly easy to do and free and it will show your initiative. Remember to keep anything you produce professional and try to build up a varied portfolio to showcase a range of talents.

The Personal Statement

Admissions tutors want to know:

- Why you are applying to study Journalism/Media. Many people think that these are glamorous industries but this is rarely the case, especially when you are starting out. Try to show an awareness of the reality of the hard work involved and your dedication to the industry.
- What have you done to explore the study of Journalism/Media outside of school or in other subjects? As explained above, you

should aim to gain work experience or create your own media. You should also show how you have engaged with established media products. This is a must-have as it proves your genuine interest in the subject and that you are capable of independent work.
- Any fields of Journalism/Media that you are interested in and why. These degrees are very broad and you will be expected to work on several different kinds of projects so you should try to show that you are open to all aspects of the industry in your application, however if there are any specialist areas that you have a particular passion for, you should mention them.
- What you intend to do after studying this degree (if you have any plans).
- What makes you well prepared for studying a degree in general? Talk about any jobs, extra-curricular or other activities that you have done which show you have the skills necessary to do well at university.

Remember that admissions tutors will be looking for evidence of how well you write, so it is imperative that your personal statement has no mistakes and a good flow to it.

Music

If you wish to study Music you have the option of attending a university where you will normally receive a BA.(Mus), "Bachelor of Arts degree in Music", or a conservatoire where you will normally receive a BMus, "Bachelor of Music". Both are recognized undergraduate degrees but the BA is less specialised and can be about a wide range of musically related topics, whereas the BMus degree is more about performance or composition. If you are applying to a BA degree it will be through UCAS, if you are applying for a BMus it will be through CUKAS (cukas.ac.uk), unless you are applying to Guildhall school of Music and Drama whereby it is required to apply directly to the school.

Career destinations

With a degree in music, there is no obvious jump from degree to employment, as there might be with a more vocational subject.

There are a number of career options for those wishing to continue working in the music industry. These include pursuing a career as a professional performer or composer, working in music production, music theatre, or arts media, and working with children or other groups of people. Each option will require a different path after the Music degree, for example those aiming to become professional performers will likely complete a fourth year at a conservatoire, those interested in musicology or composition would benefit from a Masters degree, and many others will go directly into an internship or paid job with an orchestra or publisher.

For those who complete the degree and then wish to follow a career unrelated to music, they will have a received a strong base to then pursue any path whether it be law, accountancy, teaching or many others. A degree in Music will demonstrate that you have intelligence and creativity, that you have a high capacity for hard work and are open to new ideas, and that you have a high standard of professional skills such as time management, the ability to give a public presentation, and the capacity to prepare documents to a high standard.

Entry Requirements

You will typically need to have completed an A-Level in Music and have achieved Grade VII or VIII in your main instrument. Some Universities prefer you to have completed at least one essay based subject for A-Level, such as History or English.

As a Music degree is not directly related to a single vocation, it can be difficult to get work experience before starting the course. It will however be vital to demonstrate your dedication to the subject by showing that you have performed in various orchestras, theatre groups, bands etc. If you are entering the degree with a clear knowledge of the path you will follow after then work experience in this area, be it teaching, event management, or anything else, will be valuable.

Personal statements and interviews

Admissions tutors want to know:

- Your level of Keyboard playing as many Universities have a compulsory "Keyboard Skills" course.
- How you came to be interested in music and how you came to play your principal instrument, or how you came to compose or to conduct.
- Your musical interests. Are you a performer, composer, conductor, or are you wanting to teach music? What styles of music interest you? What is it about these styles that fascinate you? Extra-curricular activities. It is important to only list the most significant ones such as competition wins, big ensembles you have played in, or things you have organised or had a leading role in.

If you are applying through both UCAS and CUKAS, it could be useful to write two slightly different statements. Universities will want to get more of a sense of your whole character, while conservatoires will require more detail about performing activities and competition wins.

English and other academic subjects

English and other academic courses are essay-based and involve analysing texts in detail, applying critical interpretations and presenting arguments in writing. Assessment methods usually involve coursework and written exams, and possibly presentations. Teaching is conducted through lectures, small seminars and workshops, allowing regular individual feedback. There is a strong emphasis on independent reading and research. These subjects are often highly popular and oversubscribed, although combined courses such as English with a Foreign Language may be less competitive.

Career destinations

English and academic courses provide students with transferable skills that make them highly employable, including excellent written and oral communication skills, cultural awareness and the ability to analyse and critically evaluate information, as well as work independently. They typically go on to work in professions such as academia, teaching, law, business and finance, public administration, non-governmental organisations, journalism and publishing, libraries and museums. Many academic students also go on to further study.

Most universities make the majority of their offers on the basis of students' UCAS applications alone. However, Oxford and Cambridge require students to sit an additional written test and UCL and Warwick invite applicants to interview, while York interviews mature students. As these are essay-based degrees, a well-written literary personal statement is essential. However, do not think of your personal statement like a novel or a piece of prose. It is a piece of writing with a specific function and purpose as described in the personal statement section of this book.

Entry requirements

English and academic degree entry requirements vary from A*AA-DDC depending on the university you apply to. Some universities state that they would like you to have studied a foreign language at GCSE level but all will expect you to study English Literature at A-level (or History if you are applying for History etc). Universities are generally happy to accept one less traditionally academic subject alongside two relevant academic subjects.

Work experience is not essential as there is rarely a practical work element to academic courses. However, any related work you have done should be included, of course. If you do not have any, you should be sure to include practical experiences such as visits to relevant galleries, exhibitions, plays, museums or other experiences which have broadened your understanding of the subject you are applying for.

The personal statement

Admissions tutors want to know:

- What examples and experiences do you have that show your love of the subject?
- Why you are applying to study English (or another academic subject). Remember that admissions tutors will read hundreds of personal statements so try to keep yours very focused.
- What further reading you have done. For a literature-based course, this is essential. You should talk about what writing excites you and why. You should be honest but also try to focus on examples that will make you stand out rather than the mainstream blockbuster books from that year. Discussing a particular writer or source that is not on your A level curriculum is a good idea. It is also good to show you have read a broad range of literature. If you have read any literary criticism, make sure that you mention this. It shows your genuine interest in the subject and proves that you are capable of independent work, which is useful as most academic degrees have a lot of self-learning and independent study time.

- What else you have done to explore your chosen degree outside of school or in other subjects. As covered in the work experience section, you should mention any trips or experiences which have expanded your appreciation of the subject. You can also discuss how your other studies have given you a deeper insight, for example, studying Drama may have helped you to better understand the structure of Shakespeare's plays in your English Literature course.
- Any fields of the subject that you are interested in and why. Try looking at the course content of your chosen universities and highlight areas which particularly appeal to you and you are keen to explore further, explaining why this is the case.
- Evidence that you think analytically and can critically evaluate sources.
- What you intend to do after studying this degree, if you have any plans. Try to show how this degree fits into your long-term ambitions and why the skills and experience you have gained will benefit you.
- What makes you well prepared for studying a degree in general? Talk about any jobs, extra-curricular or other activities that you have done which show you have the skills necessary to do well at university.

Foreign languages

Studying a foreign language at University is a very popular choice, as anyone able to speak another language automatically has increased employability. Learning a language takes a lot of hard work and discipline which is a quality highly valued by employers. The courses offered range from standard languages such as French and German to more specialised courses, for example Swahili, Somali, or Hausa.

Career destinations

The most common careers where language skills are directly utilised include translation, research, interpretation and education. Postgraduate courses in these areas, and in linguistics, are especially popular.

A degree in foreign languages will also be looked at highly in many other jobs or further study. For example;

- The advertising, marketing and PR sectors require great communication skills.
- For international charities or organisations it is often practical to employ someone who can speak more than one language.
- In law, language skills are highly valued
- Accountancy and professional services are now truly international fields.

Academic Requirements

The academic requirements vary greatly between Universities and for the language you are choosing to study. Many courses do require you to have an A-level in the language you are applying for, however others will teach from scratch, especially if it is a more specialised language such as Swahili or Chinese.

Work Experience

It will obviously be difficult to get any significant work experience in a language that you do not yet know, however it will be vital to show both your interest in that particular language, and your ability to really focus and work hard as learning a language takes a lot of dedication.

It could be valuable to demonstrate that you have spent a considerable amount of time in the area of the language you have chosen, or that you have undertaken some work experience involving knowledge of some aspect of the country, the people, or the culture. If you have a clear idea of the path you wish to follow after completing this degree, such as education, international charity work, or translation, then it will be important to gain some work experience in this area.

The personal statement

Admissions tutors want to know:

- Why you want to study this particular language. Do you have a special interest in the country and the culture?
- If you will be able to handle the demands of the course. Learning a language will take a lot of dedication and will require many hours of study outside of class time. Can you demonstrate that you have the commitment and enthusiasm to put in the work?
- What have you done to introduce yourself to the language before you begin at University? Have you started teaching yourself basic grammar? Have you been to an area where the language is spoken and picked up some useful phrases?
- If you have a career in mind after the degree. Have you thought about how fluency in this language will help you in finding work after University?

Teaching

Teaching is an extremely rewarding and satisfying career. It provides you with the opportunity to make a positive contribution to the lives of young people, everyday, which is why some teachers find that their students remember them for years to come. Each day is unique. Each child is unique. And you will spend much of your day interacting with others, which is great, especially if you're a people person. Nothing can beat the satisfaction of seeing students have that 'eureka moment' and/or achieve their goals. Some individuals are drawn to teaching due to the large amount of paid holidays this job offers, but the life of a teacher is also tough. It includes getting to school well before the students get there and leaving well after they leave. It involves planning, marking, delivering lessons, break duties, lunch duties, setting and marking tests, creating displays, attending meetings, contacting parents, dealing with the personal issues some of your students may face at home, writing reports, preparing for observations, organising assemblies, managing behaviour . . . the list could go on and on. I can tell you that from the moment you enter those doors you will be inundated with things to do and by the time you get to that half term, you will be exhausted and definitely deserve the break. However, depending on your personality, it can be one of the most rewarding and satisfying jobs you could do. Every day is a new challenge. There a number of routes into the teaching profession and we will discuss each in turn below.

Initial teacher training (ITT)

This is a university led route into teaching for those who do not have a degree level qualification. You would select one of the following courses:

Bachelor of Arts (BA) or Bachelor of Science (BSc)

A BA or BSc allows you to specialise in a certain subject (for example, maths, English, computing etc). Once you have completed the course, you will have achieved a degree and qualified teacher status (QTS). This is a popular choice for those who want to teach at secondary schools or colleges.

Bachelor of Education (BEd)

This is a popular choice for those interested in teaching primary school children. This is an honours degree course in education.

These are 3 or 4 year degrees, applied to through UCAS. Students are expected to complete a number of teaching placements, attend lectures, seminars and submit a number of assessments throughout their course. At university you will be taught the theory behind education including key terminology, government legislation and policy as well as top tips for the classroom.

Whilst on teaching placements, you are expected to put these principles into practice by planning and delivering lessons that meet the needs of the national curriculum. After most lessons, especially those that make up your assessments, you will be provided with some feedback from a subject mentor. This is a teacher at your placement school who is paid to provide you with guidance and support. This course is known to be quite intense and difficult as students have to manage the deadlines set by their university whilst planning and delivering lessons, marking work, creating displays, planning trips etc. Nevertheless, it thoroughly prepares you for the life of a teacher.

Throughout your course, you are expected to show evidence that you can meet the national teaching standards. You can find these on the department of education website.

In the final year of your course, you are encouraged to look for and apply for jobs and will consequently be booking off time to attend interviews. Your university will help you, as it is important to them that most of their students secure a teaching job after graduation.

Funding

Depending on your household income, you may find that you are eligible for a non-repayable maintenance grant, so go to the department of education website to find out more.

Work experience

Work experience is essential for any teaching course. You can write to primary or secondary schools and ask if you can come and observe lessons or shadow a teacher because you are interested in teaching. It is sometimes helpful to approach schools that you already have a link with although most schools are happy to allow students to come in. Ensure you make a note of what you have learnt from your work experience placements, as this information will be vital for your personal statement and interview.

PGCE

This is the most popular route into teaching. You can apply to this course via UCAS only after you have completed an undergraduate degree. The course structure is the same as that of the BA in education however the PGCE is only one year long (full time) and is therefore more intense.

Funding

There is currently a national shortage for science, maths, computing and languages teachers. Consequently, you may find that you are eligible for a grant to help cover part or all of the cost of your course if you are training to teach these subjects. Use the department of education website to find out more about funding.

School direct programme

The school direct programme is a school led training programme and is a relatively new route into teaching. You will spend most of your time learning on the job, planning lessons, marking work, teaching classes and will be expected to complete modules outside of classroom. There are two training options:

1) School direct salaried: if you are a highly experienced graduate with at least three years work experience in a school, you can earn a salary whilst training to become a teacher.

2) School direct: this training option is for high quality graduates who want to learn on the job. You will not be paid whilst you train and would have to pay for the course yourself however you may be eligible for a scholarship or bursary whilst you train.

SKITT (school based learning programme.

This another school led training programme in which students are taught by experienced and practising teachers within a consortium of schools. You will be taught theories and be given an opportunity to put theory intro practice within the classroom.

You can apply to the schools direct or SKITT training programmes through UCAS. As with the PGCE, you may find that you are eligble for a bursary or a grant to help cover the cost of your course. You can use the department of education website to find out more information.

Many students choose the SKITT or schools direct programme because they enjoy learning on the job. For others, the finanicial incentive of a salary on the schools direct programme entices them to apply for this style of course. Consequently, it can be quite competitive to get onto these training programmes and therefore universities often favour the most experienced and academically able candidates. The courses are very demanding as students are expected to fulfil many of the duties of a qualified teacher which include plan and deliver a large number of lessons (more than that required in PGCE or BA education courses), mark work, plan trips, makes displays, complete assignments and attend lectures or seminars outside of school hours.

Teach first

Teach first is an intense 2 year teacher training programme for graduates. In the first year, you will be paid the wage of an unqualified teacher and given 6 weeks of intense training to prepare you for the classroom. You will then start work as a teacher, in a tough school, situated in a low income area. You will have a slightly reduced teaching timetable but will still be expected to plan, deliver lessons and fulfill the responsibilities of a qualified teacher whilst completing learning modules. In your second year, you will obtain NQT status and will thus be paid the salary of a qualified teacher. You will again be expected to fulfil the responsibilites of a teacher whilst completing learning modules. At the end of the two-year course, you may decide you want to carry on teaching and stay within the profession. Or you may decide that you want to use the skills you have developed to gain entry into another profession. Either way, teach first trainees are provided with professional development, coaching and networking opportunities after they have completed their two years of training.

The teach first scheme is a very demanding and competitive course and you will be placed in some of the most difficult schools in the country. However, it is immensely rewarding and after completing the course, job opportunities for qualified trainees are excellent.

Entry requirements

The entry requirements for initial teacher training degrees vary according to institution and course. If you are looking to specialise in teaching a specific subject such as Maths, you will need to have achieved a specific grade at A level. Please use your SOI to find out more.

To get a place on the PGCE course, you need to have achieved a minimum of a C in GCSE English and Maths and at least a 2:2 in your undergraduate degree.

The Schools direct prorgramme, SKITT and Teach first programmes favour students who have achieved a minimum of a 2:1 in their undergraduate degree course.

Personal statements

Admissions tutors are looking for well-rounded individuals who have a realistic perception of the life of a teacher.

Your personal statement should focus on why you want to go into teaching and what you have learnt from your work experience placements. Admissions tutors want applicants with passion, drive and those who genuinely care about the wellbeing of young people. They are looking for applicants who can communicate effectively and have experience in managing a large number of children so write as many examples of this as you can. There are a few 'buzzwords' in teaching at the moment and it might be useful to think about whether you observed these concepts in action in your work experience. Firstly, differentiation is the ability to cater for children who have different levels of academic ability. Behaviour management is also important, as the behaviour of children can be one of the biggest barriers to learning and one of the greatest sources of stress for teachers. Another concept is assessment for learning, which refers to checking that the children are learning throughout the lesson.

Interview

The interview process is different for each course however here are some things you may be asked to do:

1. Prepare a lesson that teaches a part of the curriculum. You may be asked to deliver it to students, or explain your lesson to an interview panel. To get this right, practice your lesson with friends over and over again under timed conditions. Ensure that your lesson has clear lesson objectives that can be measured, that you have catered for children of different abilities (i.e. stretched those of a high academic ability and supported those of a low academic ability) and that you have checked the understanding of the children throughout the lesson.
2. You may be asked to partake in a group interview in which you have to discuss a key issue in education. Ensure you keep up to date with new developments in education. During the interview, speak clearly and concisely and contribute to the discussion.
3. During individual interviews you may be asked about aspects of your personal statement and why you want to become a teacher. Be honest and try to focus on the skills that you have gained that would make you an invaluable student on their course and a good teacher in the future.
4. The admissions tutors may want to assess your subject knowledge so they may set you a written assessment. It is difficult to prepare for this as each institution uses its own unique test.

Post-graduate courses

Post-graduate degrees are more specialised than undergraduate degrees and therefore there is huge variety of the types of application forms and what admissions tutors are looking for. Applications are made direct to the university department and are not generally processed through UCAS. Here are our top tips for post graduate application personal statements:

1. Know what you are supposed to show them.

Post-graduate admissions tutors usually want a personal statement, at least one reference and may require other specific details or work as part of their application forms. This information varies and will be listed on their websites.

2. Know what they are looking for.

Admissions tutors will invariably tell you what they want you to write in the personal statement or other parts of the application form. Read the information and give them what they want to hear. For example, you may have some really interesting project work you think shows off your talents, but if they say they only want to know about your reading around the topic, you should stick to writing just that.

3. Demonstrate an interest in the subject and a commitment to studying it.

People who choose to study a subject in further depth at post-graduate level usually have a strong interest in that topic and you need to prove that this applies to you. What initially got you interested in the topic? What did you do at undergraduate level that made you even more interested and committed to this topic? And crucially, what have you done outside of the undergraduate curriculum to explore this topic? Have you done any broader reading or projects and if so, how did this motivate you towards studying the topic further at post-graduate level?

4. How does this post-graduate course fit in your plans and objectives?

Admissions tutors expect a more mature approach to post-graduate applications and like to see applicants who have clear objectives for their further study or career. They like to see evidence of what you have done to pursue these goals, so just saying that you want to become CEO of a large private finance corporation is not good enough; you need to show that you have done something substantial to achieve your goals.

5. Anything you achieved more than 3-4 years ago is probably only worth a brief mention at most.

Do not spend too much time talking about old achievements such as being in the school cricket team unless they are really very impressive. Admissions tutors want to know about you more recent achievements.

A final note from the author

I wish you all the best of luck with your university application. I hope that the guidance in this book is useful for you. If you have any questions, feel free to email us at info@personalstatementchecker.com. Our team are more than happy to offer individual advice. Please also check out our website www.PersonalStatementChecker.com where our team of experts will be able to go through your personal statement in a lot more detail providing you with the level of support you deserve.

All material in this book is intended for general guidance. This book is specifically intended to substitute or supplement the advice expected to be provided by school teachers or careers advisors to individuals applying to university in the UK. As such, the author or PersonalStatementChecker.com will not be held liable for any loss, expense or misfortune experienced by those reading this book.